ABANDONED!
Towns Without People

SALTON SEA RESORT
Death in the Desert

by Kevin Blake

Consultant: Jennie Kelly
Director, Salton Sea History Museum
North Shore, California

BEARPORT
PUBLISHING

www.bearportpublishing.com

Credits:
Cover and title page, © Christian Kemp/Alamy and © Triff/Shutterstock; 4–5, © kojihirano/Shutterstock; 5T, © gabriel12/Shutterstock; 6, © Richard Broadwell/Alamy; 7, U.S. National Archives and Records Administration; 8, Courtesy of The Imperial Irrigation District; 9, © Phil Konstantin/tinyurl.com/n2wzv6a/ CC BY 2.0; 11T, Courtesy of the Coachella Valley Historical Society; 11B, Courtesy of the Coachella Valley Historical Society; 12L, Courtesy of the Coachella Valley Historical Society; 12R, © AP Photo; 13, Courtesy of the Coachella Valley Historical Society; 14–15, © welcomia/Shutterstock; 16, © Daniel Mayer/tinyurl.com/nongt6y/CC BY-SA 3.0; 17L, © Christina Lange/Alamy; 17R, Courtesy of the Salton Sea History Museum; 18–19, © AP Photo/Nick Ut; 19R, © AP Photo/Press Enterprise/Jimmy Dorantes; 20, © Design Pics Inc./Alamy; 21, © Bob Reynolds/Shutterstock; 22, © Christopher Bounds/tinyurl. com/mjlqdf6/CC BY-SA 2.0; 23, © Photos 12/Alamy; 24L, © ZUMA Press, Inc./Alamy; 24–25, © Leon Werdinger/Alamy; 26, © gabriel12/Shutterstock; 27T, © Colin Brown/tinyurl.com/nfsnkrz/CC BY 2.0; 27B, © Patty Mullins/tinyurl.com/kzynaxz/CC BY 2.0; 28, Courtesy of the Coachella Valley Historical Society; 29T, © Design Pics Inc./Alamy; 29B, © kojihirano/Shutterstock.

Publisher: Kenn Goin
Editor: Jessica Rudolph
Creative Director: Spencer Brinker
Design: The Design Lab
Photo Researcher: Jennifer Zeiger

Library of Congress Cataloging-in-Publication Data

Blake, Kevin, 1978–
  Salton Sea resort : death in the desert / by Kevin Blake.
     pages cm. — (Abandoned! : towns without people)
  Includes bibliographical references and index.
  ISBN 978-1-62724-523-4 (library binding)—ISBN 1-62724-523-5 (library binding)
  1. Salton Sea (Calif.)—History—Juvenile literature. 2. Ghost towns—California—Juvenile literature.
  3. Salton Sea (Calif.)—Environmental conditions—Juvenile literature. 4. Landscape changes—California—Salton Sea—Juvenile literature. I. Title.
  F868.I2B53 2015
  979.4'99—dc23
                                    2014036566

For more information, write to Bearport Publishing Company, Inc., 45 West 21st Street, Suite 3B, New York, New York 10010. Printed in the United States of America.

10 9 8 7 6 5 4 3 2 1

Contents

Not What It Seems

From far away, the Salton Sea looks like a paradise. California's largest lake is surrounded by a white beach and red mountains. Birds glide above the cool, crisp blue water looking for fish to eat. It seems like the perfect place for people to enjoy a sunny vacation.

The Salton Sea

The Salton Sea is actually a lake. People probably started calling it a sea because of its very large size.

A closer look, however, reveals the truth about the Salton Sea. The sand is actually covered with **barnacle** shells and the bones of dead fish. The water isn't always blue. Sometimes it turns green or brown. At one time, hundreds of thousands of people crowded the lake and its beaches each year. Now, many areas around the lake are **abandoned**. What happened to the once-thriving Salton Sea?

Fish bones on the beach of the Salton Sea

Disappearing Lakes

Change isn't new to the Salton Sea. In fact, there have been many times in the past when there was no lake in that area at all. For the last 10,000 years, lakes have been forming and then disappearing in the Salton **Basin**—one of the lowest points in the United States. Occasionally, **floods** filled the bowl-shaped area with water, creating a lake. Then, over time, the extreme summer heat—reaching over 120°F (49°C)—would cause the water to **evaporate** and disappear.

The bottom of the Salton Sea is 278 feet (85 m) below **sea level**. That's only 4 feet (1.2 m) higher than Death Valley—the lowest spot in the United States.

The hot California sun can cause lakes to evaporate.

Recently, people have played a part in creating a lake in the basin. In 1901, **canals** were dug in the area for farmers who needed water for their crops. These narrow waterways directed some water from the Colorado River toward farms. However, things didn't go as planned. In 1905, the Colorado River flooded. Water poured through the canals into the Salton Basin. The flood was so powerful that water burst through the canal walls.

This canal, built in the 1930s, takes water from the Colorado River to farms in California.

A Giant Lake

For months, water from the Colorado River spilled into the basin. Huge waterfalls—up to 80 feet (24 m) high—ripped through farmland and crashed down into a quickly growing lake. The farmers now had a new problem. They needed to stop the raging river that was destroying their crops.

Floodwaters pour into the Salton Basin area in the early 1900s.

Soon, thousands of railroad cars were carrying gravel, wood, and clay to the basin. Almost 2,000 construction workers used these materials to build walls to stop the flow of water. Finally, in 1907, the work was done and the flood ended. What remained was the biggest lake in California—the Salton Sea.

The new lake measured about 45 miles (72 km) long and 17 miles (27 km) wide—bigger than the entire city of San Diego, California.

Growing Towns

It didn't take long for **tourists** to discover the beautiful new lake in an area with year-round sunny skies. Families in Los Angeles and San Diego began to drive to the Salton Sea. They relaxed on the beach or escaped the heat by taking a dip in the cool water.

The Salton Sea is about 120 miles (193 km) from San Diego and 150 miles (241 km) from Los Angeles. These are California's two largest cities.

In the 1950s, when air-conditioning became more common, **real-estate developers** saw an opportunity to make money by attracting even more people to the Salton Sea. They built hotels and restaurants for vacationers. The developers also spent millions of dollars to create new **resort** towns, such as Bombay Beach and Salton City. Shops and schools were constructed to encourage families to move to the desert. With air-conditioning in many of the new buildings, people could enjoy the Salton Sea even during the hottest months.

Postcards from the Salton Sea show people having fun at the beach.

The Salton Sea was **stocked** with many kinds of fish, such as corvina and Gulf croaker, so tourists could go fishing. Birds began flying to the lake to feed on the fish.

Stars in the Sun

The Salton Sea was not just for ordinary families. Only a few hours' drive away from Hollywood, the lake became a popular vacation spot for movie stars and musicians. Developers built expensive hotels and **yacht** clubs for celebrities. Stars like Frank Sinatra and the Beach Boys enjoyed boating and swimming in the sparkling waters along with everyone else.

Frank Sinatra

Visitors came from all over to enter boat races at the lake.

The chance to meet the rich and famous only made the Salton Sea more popular. For years, the towns were very successful. What had started as an accidental lake was now known as the "West's Greatest Playground." It looked like nothing could stop the Salton Sea's success. However, something terrible was happening beneath the lake's surface.

In the 1950s and 1960s, up to 500,000 tourists visited the Salton Sea each year.

Runoff

While people happily swam and lay out in the sun, farmers near the lake worked the land. They sprayed water and **fertilizers** onto fields to help their crops grow. The water and fertilizer chemicals **seeped** into the ground and mixed with salt in the soil. This blend of water, chemicals, and salt—called runoff—trickled down into the Salton Sea.

Runoff in the Salton
Sea comes from farms
in Southern California.

Each year, the blazing hot sun evaporated more and more water in the Salton Sea. The chemicals and salt in the runoff, however, did not evaporate. Slowly, the Salton Sea began to change.

Approximately 4 million tons (3.6 million metric tons) of salt from farm runoff enter the lake every year.

A Slimy, Salty Lake

In the early 1970s, people began to notice changes in the lake. Swimmers passed by globs of green **algae** floating in the water. Fertilizers in the runoff actually helped this thick, green slime grow. Sometimes the algae would cause the water to change color from blue to green or brown.

Algae in the Salton Sea can occasionally give off a terrible smell.

Swimmers also noticed that the water tasted different. What used to be fresh water became salty from the tons of salt being fed into the lake each year. Clumps of salt would even form on the beach.

Today, the Salton Sea is about 50 percent saltier than the Pacific Ocean.

Piles of salt in the Salton Sea

Wildlife Graveyard

The changes in the water created horrible problems for the lake's wildlife. Algae used up much of the oxygen in the water. With little oxygen left, many fish could not breathe and drowned. Their bodies washed up onto the shore and **decayed** in the sun. The beaches became a huge fish graveyard.

Fish in the Salton Sea died from a lack of oxygen, as well as from the extreme amount of salt in the lake.

Spotting an easy meal, birds swooped down to feed on the dead, rotting fish. Unfortunately, many of these fish carried a deadly disease called **botulism**, which was passed on to the hungry birds. Dying birds piled up on the beach next to the fish. The paradise had turned into a nightmare.

A dead bird at the Salton Sea

Since the 1970s, millions of birds and fish have died at the Salton Sea.

Abandoned

By the late 1970s, the situation at the Salton Sea had gotten even worse. Floods destroyed parts of many of the towns along the shore. Because of all the problems at the lake, vacationers stopped coming to the Salton Sea. This was a disaster for towns like Bombay Beach that depended on tourists. Many people who worked in the tourism industry lost their jobs and left town.

Floods destroyed some areas of Bombay Beach. The ruined areas were never rebuilt.

Today, there are very few people living in Bombay Beach. Motels, yacht clubs, and other businesses stand empty. There are no longer any gas stations, so people often drive around in electric golf carts. To get groceries, they have to drive 40 miles (64 km) away. Celebrities don't visit anymore, and Bombay Beach is now one of the poorest towns in Southern California.

Only 295 people live in Bombay Beach today.

Motels and other businesses built during the Salton Sea's busy years have since been abandoned.

Picturing What's Left

Today, Bombay Beach gets only a few visitors every year. Most of them are photographers who come to take pictures of the town's destruction. The artists' photos show that the community has become a **ghost town**. Homes purchased in the 1950s are littered with piles of trash. The signs for motels have crumbled and the yacht clubs have been painted over with **graffiti**. Empty fishing boats float quietly in the sea.

This abandoned home has almost completely fallen apart.

In the center of Bombay Beach, photographers climb over **rubble** to snap pictures of a rusted metal trailer. It used to be a mobile home, but now it's hard to tell what it was. The trailer, like much of the town, is slowing sinking into an enormous puddle of **sludge**.

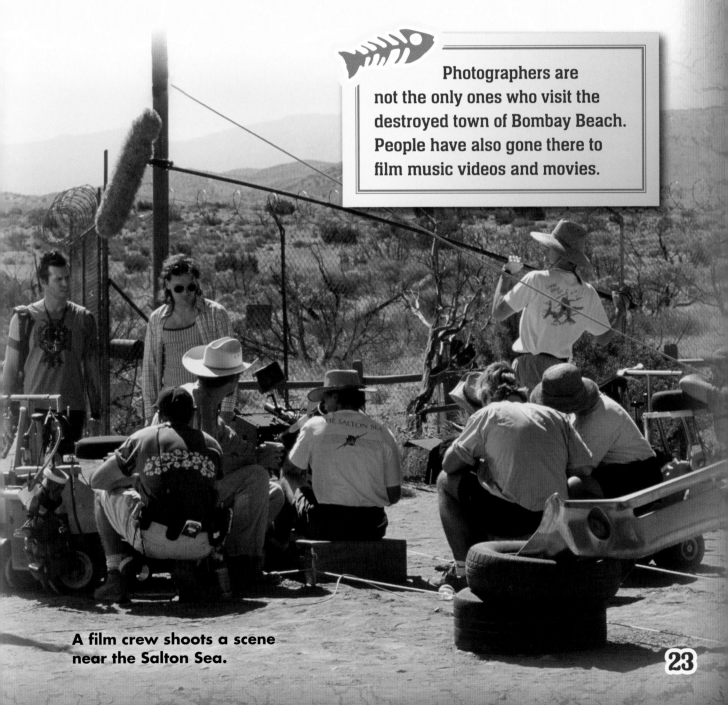

Photographers are not the only ones who visit the destroyed town of Bombay Beach. People have also gone there to film music videos and movies.

A film crew shoots a scene near the Salton Sea.

Toxic Cloud

After seeing the destruction that the flooding, algae, and high salt levels have caused at the Salton Sea, some people have offered a solution: Why not direct the farm runoff somewhere else? Then the lake would dry up and disappear. Unfortunately, this would create another disaster. Why?

Much of this lake in eastern California has evaporated. Many people do not want the same thing to happen to the Salton Sea.

Most of the chemicals from the runoff have settled at the bottom of the lake. Without water to weigh the chemicals down, they could dry up and be carried away by the wind. The wind could then blow a **toxic** cloud toward Los Angeles and San Diego. Even now, a small portion of the lake has evaporated, and nearby farmers sometimes get a whiff of the chemicals in the air. The effect can be very unhealthy. Farmer Al Kalin said, "This white dust we have—it burns your eyes, it burns your nose [and] your throat."

Farmers like Al Kalin (above) worry about dried-up toxic chemicals being blown toward farms and towns.

Breathing in runoff chemicals could cause serious diseases like asthma and cancer.

The Future of the Salton Sea

There's another reason many people don't want the Salton Sea to dry up. It's true that some towns along the shore have been destroyed. However, other parts of the giant lake are still a paradise, especially for wildlife. Land along the southern end of the Salton Sea has been set aside as a wildlife **refuge**. Millions of birds find food and raise their young there.

Hundreds of different kinds of birds make their home at the Salton Sea wildlife refuge, including pelicans (below), egrets, and owls.

Today, scientists are developing a plan to make the lake an even better home for wildlife. The newest technology is able to remove much of the salt from the water. This will make it safer for the remaining fish. Fixing the lake won't happen overnight. Fortunately, though, many people are working to make the Salton Sea better for tomorrow.

A kayaker

People fishing at the lake

Despite its **reputation** as a **polluted** lake, thousands of people come to the Salton Sea every year to enjoy outdoor activities. Visitors can fish, swim, bird watch, hike, and go boating and kayaking.

The Salton Sea: Then and Now

THEN: Hollywood celebrities vacationed at the Salton Sea in the 1950s and 1960s.

NOW: The Salton Sea is one of the poorest areas in California.

THEN: Fishermen caught corvina and other types of fish.

NOW: Much of the corvina died off due to changes in the water.

THEN: The Salton Sea hosted boat races.

NOW: Boats sit empty, bobbing in the lake.

THEN: Developers built new towns like Bombay Beach to house the people who wanted to live near the lake.

NOW: Most people have left these towns. Only 295 people are living in Bombay Beach.

THEN: The Salton Sea was a freshwater lake.

NOW: The lake is about 50 percent saltier than the Pacific Ocean.

GLOSSARY

abandoned (uh-BAN-duhnd) empty, no longer used

algae (AL-jee) tiny plantlike living things often found in lakes, ponds, and other bodies of water

barnacle (BAR-nuh-kuhl) a saltwater creature that, as an adult, is permanently fastened to something such as a rock or the bottom of a ship

basin (BAY-sin) a sunken part of the earth, sometimes shaped like a bowl

botulism (BOCH-yuh-*liz*-uhm) a deadly disease caused by eating food that contains a certain bacteria

canals (kuh-NALZ) channels, or narrow stretches of water, that are dug across land

decayed (di-KAYD) rotted

evaporate (i-VAP-uh-rayt) to dry up; to change from a liquid into a gas

fertilizers (FUR-tuh-*lize*-urz) substances used to help make soil richer so crops will grow

floods (FLUHDZ) overflows of water onto land

ghost town (GOHST TOUN) a town, once lived in, where almost everyone has left but the buildings still stand

graffiti (gruh-FEE-tee) pictures or words made on a building or other surface, usually without permission

polluted (puh-LOOT-id) dirty, due to harmful materials, such as chemicals, being added to air, soil, or water

real-estate developers (REEL-ess-*tayt* di-VEL-uh-purz) people who construct and sell buildings

refuge (REF-yooj) a place that protects animals or people

reputation (rep-yoo-TAY-shuhn) the opinion that most people have about a person, place, or thing

resort (ri-ZORT) a place where people on vacation relax and have fun

rubble (RUHB-uhl) piles of things that have been broken or destroyed

sea level (SEE LEV-uhl) the average height of the world's sea surface

seeped (SEEPD) flowed slowly through small openings

sludge (SLUDJ) a thick, soft mud, often mixed with chemicals

stocked (STOKT) filled with a supply of something

tourists (TOOR-ists) people who are traveling on vacation

toxic (TOK-sik) poisonous, deadly

yacht (YOT) a large, expensive boat

BIBLIOGRAPHY

Bourne, Joel, Jr. "Salton Sea," *National Geographic Magazine* (February 2005).

Morton, Ella. "Salton Sea: From Relaxing Resort to Skeleton-Filled Wasteland," *Slate* (February 4, 2014).

Stringfellow, Kim. *Greetings from the Salton Sea: Folly and Intervention in the Southern California Landscape, 1905–2005 (Center Books on American Places)*. Santa Fe, NM: Center for American Places (2005).

READ MORE

Ansary, Mir Tamim. *All Around California: Regions and Resources (Heinemann State Studies)*. Chicago, IL: Heinemann (2003).

Duffield, Katy. *California History for Kids: Missions, Miners, and Moviemakers in the Golden State*. Chicago, IL: Chicago Review (2012).

Rice, William B. *Death Valley Desert (TIME for Kids Nonfiction Readers)*. Huntington Beach, CA: Teacher Created Materials (2012).

LEARN MORE ONLINE

To learn more about the Salton Sea, visit
www.bearportpublishing.com/Abandoned

INDEX

ABOUT THE AUTHOR

Kevin Blake has written several books for children.
He lives in Portland, Oregon—not a ghost town!—
with his wife, Melissa, and son, Sam.

DATE DUE